Joel,

To the special
Daddy to our grandchildren
We are thankful each day that
you are our son-in-law and the
girls father! Love
Grant & Nancy

D1042334

The Miracle in a
Daddy's
Hug

The Miracle in a
Daddy's
Hug

John Burns

HOWARD PUBLISHING CO.

OUR PURPOSE AT HOWARD PUBLISHING IS TO:

- *Increase faith* in the hearts of growing Christians
- *Inspire holiness* in the lives of believers
- *Instill hope* in the hearts of struggling people everywhere

BECAUSE HE'S COMING AGAIN!

The Miracle in a Daddy's Hug © 2003 by John Burns
All rights reserved. Printed in the United States of America
Published by Howard Publishing Co., Inc.
3117 North 7th Street, West Monroe, Louisiana 71291-2227

03 04 05 06 07 08 09 10 11 12   10 9 8 7 6 5 4 3 2 1

Edited by Michele Buckingham
Interior design by Stephanie D. Walker

Library of Congress Cataloging-in-Publication Data
Burns, John, 1953-
    The miracle in a daddy's hug / John Burns.
        p. cm.
    Includes bibliographical references.
    ISBN 1-58229-331-7
    1. Fathers. 2. Father and child. 3. Love. 4. Spiritaul life. I. Title.

HQ756.B87 2003
306.874'2—dc22

                                        2003059542

contents

The Miracle in a Daddy's Hug

I was standing by the kitchen counter when my daughter Danica entered the room. I couldn't help but notice the pained look on her face. Obviously unhappy with herself, she avoided my glance and pretended to be busy, arranging and rearranging the settings on the table. As I watched her, I prayed silently, *God, show me how to help her.*

Danica was wasting away before my eyes. The second of my three wonderful daughters, she had developed an eating disorder when she was about twelve years old. Several years passed before we fully understood what the problem was. By that time her condition was serious.

I took the typical male approach and tried to fix it. I told her what to eat, what not to eat, when to eat, how to eat—I had all the answers. But she just got worse. Now she was eighteen, and I was desperate.

My wife, Helen, and I had been in ministry for eight years. We were the busy pastors of a growing church, the hosts of an internationally broadcast television program called *Family Success,* and regular speakers at marriage-and-family seminars. I had authored a book about parent-child relationships called *Communication Breakthrough,* and Helen had just released her own book, *Marriage, Motherhood, and Me.* People looked to us for parenting help—yet our own daughter's life was in danger. Despite all our best efforts, counsel, and prayers, Danica's health continued to deteriorate.

Finally we had to admit we had come to the end of ourselves.

It's good to come to the end of yourself, because that's where God starts.

I poured my heart out to God, pleading with him to intervene —to do something spectacular to save Danica's life. I gladly would have given up everything to see my daughter healed and well! But when I finished praying, nothing extraordinary happened. There were no lightning bolts, no angelic encounters. I simply had a new sense of confidence that Danica was going to be OK. It was as if God said, *She already has within her everything she needs to overcome her illness.* All I needed to do was to let go, stop trying to control the situation, and trust God and Danica with her future.

The sense of relief I felt was overwhelming! But now the question was, how would I get that new confidence and understanding from my heart to hers? I knew that words alone would not be enough. Danica had heard all the words. She was brilliant! She could have written her own book on how to overcome an eating disorder, on how and why to eat right. She didn't need any more information.

That's when I discovered the miracle in a daddy's hug.

I looked again at Danica from across the kitchen, and suddenly I knew what to do. Purposefully, I walked straight toward her, took her by the hand, and said, "Come here, honey. Your dad needs a hug."

I put my arms around her. She hugged me back dutifully for a second or two and then released her hold, assuming the hug was over. But I didn't let go. She fidgeted a bit in my arms.

I could almost hear her thinking, *Shouldn't this hug be finished?* Still I didn't budge. After a few clumsy moments of expecting *He'll let go any second now,* she finally got it: *He's not going to let go.* She melted into my arms like a sponge, sopping up all the love I could give, as I said, "I love you." I whispered, "I'm so proud of you. You'll always be my princess. Nothing you could ever do could make me love you more, and nothing you could ever do could make me love you less. Out of all the people in this world, God gave you to me and mom to be our daughter. You are the perfect daughter for us. You continually amaze me with how special and unique you are. Every time I see you, my heart skips with joy. I love you."

I'd like you to hear from Danica, as she tells her recollection of that moment.

> *It had been a rough day. It had been a rough year. I felt as if I had been tumbling down the side of a rocky, jagged cliff that seemed to have no end, and I was broken, exhausted, and helpless.*
>
> *I left my bedroom and headed downstairs, deep in thought. When had my world grown so dark and heavy? I was afraid, and I felt desperately alone. It startled me a*

little to find Dad in the kitchen. Our eyes met suddenly, and I knew I didn't have time to hide the fear and weariness evident in mine. What would he say? Surely he knew what my day had been like. Surely he knew the things I had done. Would he scold me and challenge me to have more faith? Would he be disgusted and shake his head? I waited for the verdict.

He motioned for me to come closer. "Come here," he said. I was torn inside. I wanted to lower my eyes and run back into the darkness to hide. But his eyes were steady and his arms were open. I could cope with scolding; the guilt was well deserved. I could understand disgust or even pity. But this looked like none of the answers I'd expected, and my heart was panicked and unsure.

He stood, patiently waiting for me to cross the distance between his arms and my small body. He wrapped his arms around me, and I was flooded with a warmth that overwhelmed me.

I pulled away after a few moments, feeling I couldn't take it anymore. But he held me even tighter, nestling my head upon his chest. It felt like an eternity, and I tried again to pull away. He didn't budge. After several futile attempts, I finally gave in. First my body gave in, and then my heart began to relax.

There was more healing to be done than could be managed in one session, but this was the start we needed. This moment communicated that I was no longer alone. Just as I was, in my broken and desperate state, I was accepted and loved.

In those few precious moments, the crisis in my daughter's life and in the life of our family turned a corner. From that point on, I knew—and Danica knew—that she would not only survive; she would overcome her challenge, regain her health, and emerge as a beautiful, victorious young woman of God.

Thank God for the miracle in a daddy's hug!

Do You Need a Miracle?

The "miracle" in *The Miracle in a Daddy's Hug* has a twofold meaning. First, a child being held in a daddy's arms is a unique and wonderful miracle of God's creation—and not just a miracle, but a miracle full of miracles still to be realized. So much life, so much potential is still ahead! Second, a daddy's embrace has miracle-working power. When a father wraps his arms, his words, his love, and his faith around his son or daughter, he opens the way for a miracle in both their lives.

There are seven components in the miracle in a daddy's hug. The first is the child—that miracle full of miracles in seed form. The second is the daddy, whose role it is to watch over and care tenderly for his miracle seed. The last five components are the nutrients in the soil that make the miracle grow: Daddy's touch, words, time, love, and faith. In the following chapters, we'll look more closely at each of these components.

My heartfelt prayer is that this book will produce miracles. I pray that each of us will discover who we are and recognize the potential God has packed within us. I pray that we will come to see fathers and fatherhood in a fresh, new way. Mostly, I pray that fathers and fathers-to-be will be encouraged and better equipped to raise their unique, God-given miracles called children.

My prayer is that this book will bring understanding and freedom to every child, provide vision and strategy for every parent, and build a sense of value and confidence in every dad. After all, each of us has a heavenly Father who longs to embrace us with his grace, his forgiveness, and his unconditional love. In his perfect, heavenly hug, we find our ultimate miracle. It is God's embrace that we as dads imitate.

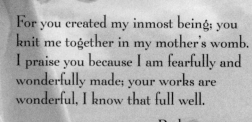

For you created my inmost being; you knit me together in my mother's womb. I praise you because I am fearfully and wonderfully made; your works are wonderful, I know that full well.

—Psalm 139:13–14

The Miracle in a Child

Every child is a miracle—an awesome miracle full of miracles still in seed form. As parents we start out in awe of this gift from heaven.

Dorothy in *The Wizard of Oz* was a little off track, I think. She was looking for a land called Oz, when she should have been looking for the land called Awe. The land of Awe is that special place—nearer than we might think—where we are continually in awe of God's miracles around us.

I once heard a great quote: "Life is not measured by how many breaths we take, but by how many times it takes our breath away." I can tell you three times that my breath has been taken away: at the births of my three daughters. Since those first moments of their lives, I have been permanently settled in the land of Awe.

Nothing compares to the wonder of a newborn child. He or she is a brand-new, eternal being, full of unlimited potential. What a weighty responsibility and sobering privilege it is to be entrusted with the care of this new little person! When we bring an infant home from the maternity ward, we immediately assume the everyday responsibility of training and equipping that child to become the best he or she can be. We enjoy the wonderful privilege of knowing and loving this new eternal being in a way no one else can. It's the beginning of a phenomenal venture of faith!

The land of Awe is the healthiest place to raise a child.

Raising Children in the Land of Awe

The land of Awe is the healthiest place to raise a child. All children learn about themselves through the eyes of their parents. When we're continually in awe of the miracles we are privileged to call our sons or daughters—when we recognize all the miracles that are hidden like treasures inside them—they can grow up seeing their own lives as miracles full of miracles.

I have often said to each of my daughters, "You're my hero. When I grow up, I want to be just like you!" I'm in awe of the miracle each one of them represents. I want them to know what I see in them, because the way children see themselves and think of themselves is the greatest determinant in who they will become and what they will accomplish in life. As Solomon wrote, "For as he thinks in his heart, so is he" (Proverbs 23:7 NKJV).

Since most of a child's self-image is developed through the eyes of Mom and Dad, we need to open our eyes and see the awesome potential God has placed in our children. Every child has awe-inspiring qualities—although it may take a purposeful effort at times to look past the not-so-perfect behavior and find the hidden treasure. Remember, what you see is what you get! As dads we need to choose to see the miracles. We need to choose to live and raise our children in the land of Awe.

Respect and Honor

Like all human beings, our children are unique, eternal individuals. Like us, they have their own private little worlds—their own thoughts, feelings, beliefs, experiences, and decisions that are taking place inside them all the time. Whether or not they share those worlds with us depends upon how much we value them as individuals and to what degree we honor and respect their private lives.

It's important that dads honor and respect their children. Moses taught that the first commandment with a promise is, "Honor your father and your mother, so that you may live long in the land the LORD your God is giving you" (Exodus 20:12). As fathers we want our children to receive God's promise. But how do we teach them to honor us so they can "live long in the land" and experience all the best God has for them?

By respecting and honoring them.

The wonderful thing about respect is that it always comes back to the one who offers it. Everyone has a need to be valued. When we value an individual—when we show respect and honor—we become valuable to that person because we're meeting a need. That person in turn treats us as valuable and shows us respect and honor. This is the kind of reciprocation that takes place between parents and children. When we treat our sons and daughters with respect and honor, they treat us with respect and honor in return, and they are set on the path toward a long and fulfilling life.

One of the best ways to show that we honor and respect our children is by valuing their thoughts and opinions. We need to listen to our kids and try to understand what they are saying. We need to thank them for sharing their hearts.

The wonderful thing about respect is that it always comes back to the one who offers it.

When children know that their fathers treasure their thoughts and opinions, a tremendous sense of self-worth is built into their lives.

The opposite is true when fathers don't value their children—when they degrade them by laughing at, disregarding, or constantly correcting their opinions and ideas. Children expect Mom and Dad to have the time and the desire to understand them, appreciate them, and treasure what they treasure. When those expectations go unmet, self-esteem plummets, and the seeds of rebellion are sown. Children who don't learn to respect and honor their parents in their early years (because their parents never respected or honored *them*) often become rebellious when they reach teen age.

We can show our children that we honor and respect them by prioritizing time for them—by setting aside time in our busy schedules to read to them, play with them, and pray with them. We can also show respect through diligently disciplining them in love and by setting and maintaining healthy behavioral boundaries. And, finally, in a book about hugging, we must include the caution that parents respect their children by *never* crossing the boundaries between proper and improper touch. The discussions in this book about the importance of showing affection must never be seen as "permission" for improper touching of any kind. Nor should parents disrespect their children by displays of "forced affection." Respect your child's comfort zones—don't make your child feel uncomfortable by forcing unwanted affection. In nurturing and loving our children, we must maintain a healthy balance between giving our children the physical affection they need and being ever careful to avoid even a hint of sexuality in the way we touch. In a child's internal vocabulary, all of these things spell *value*.

One-on-One Time with Dad

For my daughters, *value* came to be spelled T-I-M-E with D-A-D-D-Y. The idea of spending individual time with my daughters came to me when I was on my way home after another busy weekend on the road. As I hurried through the airport, I thought about how much I missed my family. My three daughters were growing up so fast—my oldest, Angela, was already eight years old—yet I was seeing less and less of them. Something needed to change! Somehow I needed to make more time for my girls.

I ducked into a card shop in the airport concourse where a children's party invitation caught my eye. It had a picture of a bright yellow sun on the front and the words "You are invited." Since Angela's middle name is Sunshine, I knew it was the perfect card for her. Feeling creative, I bought the card and filled in the blanks, inviting Angela to go on a special outing with her daddy.

She was in school when I got home, so I went into her room and left the invitation on her pillow. Later when she opened the card, she was beside herself. She could hardly wait for our special evening!

When the special day arrived, I came home from work to find Angela waiting for me. As I walked in the front door, she stepped out onto the landing at the top of the staircase. She looked like a princess. I knew she'd spent several hours fussing in front of the mirror to look "just perfect"—and her face was beaming.

Recognizing the importance of the evening, I quickly changed into my best suit. I led my daughter by the arm and opened the car door for her. We drove to the best restaurant in town, and the maître d' escorted us to a quaint, candlelit table for two.

I discovered that my daughter's world was just as important to her as mine was to me.

I purposely left behind my hats of "father," "breadwinner," and "head of the home." I simply wanted to be Angela's friend and talk with her like a friend.

But as our lovely dinner was served, the thought came to me: *Exactly how do I talk to an eight-year-old?* I was shocked to realize I had no idea of what went on in Angela's private little world. Up to that time, I had never thought to stop and ask. I guess I had regarded her world as trivial compared to my adult world of important responsibilities.

Awkwardly I began to ask questions. What subjects did she like at school? What did she do at recess? What were her friends' names? As I made my clumsy inquiries, I discovered that my daughter's world was just as important to her as mine was to me. And I discovered something else: Packaged inside the amazing little girl I was privileged to call my daughter was miracle after miracle!

That night was the beginning of a great family tradition. I began taking each girl on an individual "date" once a month. We put a big calendar on our refrigerator (at eye level for the girls), and the first activities we wrote down were always our daddy-daughter dates. The girls would walk by the refrigerator over and over again just to see their names on that calendar. They knew their special times with Dad meant they were valuable and important to him.

My wife, Helen, and I went on weekly dates—and our girls loved it. They were almost as excited about our husband-wife dates as they were about their daddy-daughter dates. There's something wonderful about knowing that your parents love one another and enjoy being together!

Of course, girls (and moms) aren't the only ones who need individual time with Dad. A son needs special, planned times with his father at least as much as his sister does. He needs to know that Dad loves him and values him enough to set aside time just for him. His confidence, security, and self-worth are dependent upon it.

A boy may not want to get gussied up and go to a fancy restaurant for a candlelit dinner. He may prefer a ball game or a trip to the pizza parlor. Ultimately, the location doesn't matter—as long as it provides an environment for healthy communication and enjoying one another's company.

When my friend Casey Treat, pastor of Christian Faith Center in Seattle, first heard me speak about "dating" my daughters, he decided to adjust the idea for his son, who was four years old at the time. Casey figured that one of the times boys and dads talk best is when they are camping, so he began planning regular father-and-son camping nights. Because his son was quite young, he sometimes built a tent in the family room and put sleeping bags inside. Then the two would "camp out" overnight. Other times he would drive to a nearby lake and set up camp. Once his son had fallen asleep, he would pick him up, drive home, and carry him up to bed.

Whatever activities we share with our children, our goal as dads is to discover the hidden treasure inside our children. Every child is a miracle full of miracles; but like treasure, those miracles are often buried deep within. To discover the seeds of those miracles takes desire, time, planning, and effort.

All fathers need to be treasure hunters. We need to make it our quest to find the miracle seeds that are planted within the hearts of our sons and daughters. When we show our children that we value and respect them enough to commit our time and attention to them, we encourage those seeds to flourish and grow.

Honor your father and your
mother, so that you may live
long in the land the LORD
your God is giving you.

—Exodus 20:12

The Miracle in a Daddy

Every child is a miracle and so is every dad. If only more dads would realize how important their role is in their children's lives!

Recently, Helen and I had the privilege of ministering at Mercy Ministries in Nashville, Tennessee. Mercy Ministries was founded in 1982 by Nancy Alcorn, who had a dream to build a home where troubled girls could discover mercy and find stability in their otherwise out-of-control world. Since opening the original Mercy House, Nancy has gone on to establish several more successful homes in the United States and two in Australia. Plans are in the works to open more homes in other countries in the future.

The Daddy Hole

When Helen and I arrived in Nashville, Nancy introduced us to the forty girls who were living at Mercy House at that time. She asked the girls to share some of their life stories with us. I have to admit, I was shocked. I had never heard such horrendous stories! Rape, incest, drug abuse, teen pregnancy, eating disorders—these girls had gone through every struggle imaginable and beyond.

The common denominator that glared out from most of the stories was what Nancy calls the "daddy hole." Most of these troubled young women had fathers who were either negative and abusive or absent from their lives, either physically or functionally.

Unfortunately, their heartache is all too common. Wherever Helen and I travel, we find people struggling with this same daddy hole. I am always amazed at the pain that erupts when this void is uncovered in a person's life. And females aren't the only ones who hurt. We've seen many a big, burly man blubber like a baby when confronting the pain of a childhood without a loving father.

At Mercy House I spoke to the girls about their God-given

needs for love, security, and affirmation; and I explained why dads are so important in meeting those needs. I wanted the girls to understand that the pain they felt was normal and not their fault. I tried to explain why our world is so messed up when it comes to fatherhood. I knew I couldn't change the past for any of these young women; but I could help them understand their past, process their feelings, and build hope for the future.

Helen and I spent three days ministering the message of *The Miracle in a Daddy's Hug* to those wonderful girls. I regarded our time at Mercy House as the supreme test of the message's validity. When I returned home, I was more convinced than ever that I must write this book. Over those three miraculous days, girls who had every earthly right to hate fathers and fatherhood experienced breakthrough! Hope was reborn in their hearts, and they began to dream anew—dreams of leading normal lives; dreams of marrying loving husbands who would become strong, healthy fathers.

Security Starts with Mom and Dad

Every child's world begins with Mom. In fact, the first nine months of a baby's existence are totally Mom. She breathes for the child, eats for the child, drinks for the child. She even fights off disease for the child. By the time this new little person is delivered through the birth canal and the umbilical cord is severed, a tremendous bond between mother and child has already been well established.

Born into a new world called family, the child discovers this world—at least initially—through Mom's eyes. The question is, what does Mom see? In a healthy family, a child is the result of a husband and wife celebrating their love for one another.

> *A father demonstrates his love for his child through the love and commitment he shows to his wife.*

That love is more than feelings; it's a commitment for a lifetime. When a mother has the security and stability of knowing that her husband loves her, supports her, and is committed to her, the child sees the world through her eyes as secure and stable.

That secure vision is the gift of a loving dad. A father demonstrates his love for his child through the love and commitment he shows to his wife. A healthy father has an inner security and stability that provides security and stability for his marriage. That in turn translates into security and stability in his child's world. A child raised in a secure, stable family environment is more likely to grow up to be a secure, stable adult—and so the cycle continues.

A Vision of Dad

Like many children, when I was young, my dad was my hero. He was the biggest, the strongest, and the smartest dad of all. When I grew up, I was going to be just like him. I wish all dads would realize how big and important their lives are in the eyes of their sons and daughters!

Children start out seeing their world through their mothers, but they learn to measure the world through their father. Who Dad is, what he does, and what he provides for the family become the boundaries of a child's vision. By looking at Dad, children conclude who they can be, what they can do, and what they can expect to have in life. Dad is the role model, the window to the world. He's the identity.

Children gain much of their vision of manhood through Dad. How Dad treats Mom, how Dad deals with difficult challenges, how Dad displays emotions—the complete picture of how Dad does life is titled "Manhood," and this portrait becomes indelibly etched on a child's subconscious.

What if that portrait is flawed? The frightening reality is that, unless purposefully changed, the vision recorded in a child's subconscious becomes the blueprint for his or her future—thus, the saying "The apple doesn't fall far from the tree." A boy who has a distant or abusive father may grow up to be distant and abusive too. His sister may grow up distrustful of men or craving male attention.

The good news is, a vision can be changed. It's possible to identify the faulty vision that's responsible for negative behavior and change that vision by replacing it with a new, healthy one. This is what I encouraged the girls at Mercy House to do. People who grow up with an unhealthy vision of family can replace that vision by surrounding themselves with healthy families. Over time, the unhealthy vision will fade, and a new vision of a healthy family will take over.

As fathers we must be responsible stewards of the visions we carry in our own hearts. Our personal visions of family and fatherhood dictate more than *our* actions; they are likely to become our children's visions and dictate *their* actions too. By making a concerted effort to identify and change our own faulty visions, we can save our children an enormous amount of pain and struggle. The work we do to replace unhealthy visions with healthy ones results not only in the betterment of our own lives; it ensures the transfer of healthy visions to our children and to our children's children, for generations to come.

Setting a Standard

Looking back, I can see that this principle of vision protected and guided my daughters through their courting years. By spending special time with my daughters from an early age and treating them with dignity and respect as they were growing up, I gave them a vision of how they should be treated in the future. I set a standard for their future relationships. When the boys came knocking, if they didn't measure up to Dad, they didn't get past the front door!

Our girls had a vision, and they expected to be treated like ladies. And as is so often true in life, what we see is what we get. Today, all our daughters have wonderful husbands who've treated them with dignity and respect from the very first date.

When it comes to the future, what we see with our eyes

closed is more significant than what we see with our eyes open. The vision in our subconscious is all-important. It paints the picture we will someday see in our conscious world. But, we can't see what we don't have. Children who grow up never seeing a healthy marriage don't know how to envision a healthy marriage for themselves.

Sadly, many girls have never seen what it means to be treated like a lady, and many sons have never witnessed gentlemanly behavior. Their futures have not been hedged with the protection of a healthy vision. Girls are left wide open for abuse and mistreatment—at the hands of boys who have never seen what it means to be a gentleman.

Building a Foundation

Of course, no one has a perfect vision. No person or family is immune from difficulties. We all face them. It's not what happens *to* us that shapes our eternity; it's what happens *in* us in response to what happens to us that counts.

When the storms of life blow, we can only be as strong as the foundation we are built on. Children depend on their parents to build that foundation. They learn to lean on what their parents lean on. The strongest foundation a daddy can give his children is a personal, growing relationship with God. When a father's inner strength is rooted in God, his kids grow up learning to live by faith, not fear. Their foundation is built securely on the Rock.

Having a strong foundation is especially important when children experience failure—and they will. Everyone falls down at some point. We all make mistakes. A father's job is not so much to teach his children not to fall; it's to teach them how to get back up again. Everyone falls, but not everyone gets back up!

> *The definition of a winner is someone who gets back up one more time than he or she falls down.*

The definition of a winner is someone who gets back up one more time than he or she falls down.

The best way to teach our children to get back up is by example. When we make mistakes, how do we recover? Do we forgive ourselves and move on? Do we accept and love ourselves in the face of our imperfections? How we view ourselves and respond after a failure will greatly affect how our children see themselves and respond when they fail. Through the reflection in our eyes, they need to see that failure is not a bad thing. It's just one further step toward success.

The Safety of Grace

Unfortunately, some dads can't accept their own imperfections, and that makes them unable to accept their children's imperfections. We can't give what we don't have. The result can be tragic. Children who grow up without a daddy's acceptance almost invariably develop a painful daddy hole. Stung by rejection, they struggle for acceptance all their lives. The only answer is grace; but if grace isn't taught and applied somewhere along life's way, the cycle of rejection may continue for generations.

Every child needs to learn and experience grace. Grace gives us the freedom to love and accept ourselves in the midst of our imperfections. A dad who never makes a mistake can never model grace. That's great news, because we all make mistakes. Each of us is a work in progress, with many opportunities to extend grace to ourselves and to others.

I've learned to take the negatives of my mistakes and turn them into the positives-of-grace lessons, both in my home and in my church. I've tried to be as real and transparent before my girls as possible—a person like them who is growing and learning all the time. That's how I try to be as a pastor too. People always seem to relate better to my failures than my successes!

Children need the security blanket of a daddy's grace. When they know it's OK to make mistakes—when they know Daddy loves them despite their imperfections—they feel settled and safe. Solomon said, "In the multitude of counselors, there is safety" (Proverbs 11:14 NKJV). Our counselors are the people we feel safe with. I've always wanted my children to feel safe enough to come to me when they need counsel; that's why I've tried to raise them in an environment of grace.

God is our role model. Not only is he the perfect heavenly Father; he is the author of grace. He loves us, warts and all. He knows our needs, and he always provides a way to meet those needs. After all, he's the one who gives a daddy the miracle of a child—and the one who gives a child the miracle of a dad.

He will cover you with his feathers, and under his wings you will find refuge; his faithfulness will be your shield and rampart.

—Psalm 91:4

The Miracle in a Daddy's Touch

As I stood in the kitchen with my arms wrapped around my fragile daughter, I sensed a miracle in the making. I could feel Danica's inner walls coming down. She was slowly releasing her grip and entrusting the protection of her bruised heart into my care. She began to drink in my strength, my confidence, and my faith.

Children feel safe when they're tenderly wrapped in the strong arms of a loving father. In that special place, there is no fear, no worry, no need to hide. Daddy's arms are all-sufficient, a source of constant strength and unconditional love. They're a shelter from the unknown and unpredictable world lurking outside their embrace.

Children find their identity at home in Daddy's arms. I remember how it felt when as a small child, my dad wrapped his big, strong hands around my little hands. All of a sudden, my world was as big and secure as my daddy's. I knew exactly who I was: I was my dad's son! And I was proud of it.

The Power of Touch

Have you seen the bumper sticker that says, "Have you hugged your child today?" Paul Planet impressively describes the value of a hug when he writes:

Hugging is healthy. It helps the immune system, cures depression, reduces stress, and induces sleep. It is invigorating, rejuvenating, and has no unpleasant side affects. Hugging is nothing less than a miracle drug.

Hugging is all natural. It's organic, naturally sweet, no artificial ingredients, nonpolluting, environmentally friendly, and it is 100 percent wholesome.

Hugging is practically perfect. No batteries to wear out, inflation-proof, nonfattening, no monthly payments, theft-proof, and nontaxable.

Hugging is an underutilized resource with magical powers. When we open our hearts and arms, we encourage others to do the same.[1]

Hugs are wonderful things—and they're free! For our children's sakes, we need to employ them more often. When hugs and other expressions of loving touch are plentiful in family relationships, kids experience healing, emotional health, and success. When loving touch is lacking, they are more prone to experience sickness, depression, and defeat.

I remember the story told in our church one Sunday by a minister from El Salvador. He and his wife were expecting a baby, but the pregnancy was cut short when their infant son was born four months premature. The little guy weighed only a couple of pounds. As they watched their tiny

> *When hugs and other expressions of loving touch are plentiful in family relationships, kids experience healing, emotional health, and success.*

newborn struggle for life, they asked the doctor, "What can we do to help him?" The wise doctor's answer was simple: "Sit by the baby's side and tenderly touch him as much as possible."

The minister and his wife followed the doctor's orders. And before their eyes, their baby began to grow stronger. He not only survived; he thrived!

The fact is, medical science has proven that premature babies who get lots of tender touch gain weight up to 47 percent faster than babies who are left alone. Eight months after birth, these children weigh more and are more advanced in mental and motor development than those who didn't receive the same amount of touch.[2]

These facts shouldn't surprise us. We all have a God-given need for tender touch.

Don't Back Away

The need for touch doesn't end when we reach a certain age. Dads especially need to understand this.

About the time my oldest daughter entered her teens, my father-in-law did a very sweet thing. Sheepishly, he approached my wife and said, "I've heard John preach for years now about dating his daughters, and I've always felt guilty that I never took you on special dates. I was wondering, if it's not too late...?"

Helen was thrilled to be asked on a date by her dad. It didn't matter that she was a fully grown woman with children of her own. Her daddy has always been her hero! On their date he took her to a nice restaurant for a special meal. There he lavished her with the praises of a loving father—the words of a grateful daddy who is both proud and amazed at the wonderful woman his daughter has become.

Then, to Helen's surprise, he asked for her forgiveness. He was sorry, he said, for backing away from her in her teenage years and not giving her the same affection he'd given her as a little girl. "As I saw you becoming a woman, I felt uncomfortable," he explained. "I didn't know where to put my arms."

When Helen came home that night and recounted the conversation, I realized that I was doing the same thing with my oldest daughter, Angela. It struck me that most fathers probably back away from their adolescent daughters in a similar way. I think there are two reasons for this.

First, the overwhelming hormonal changes of puberty have

a powerful emotional effect on a girl, and most dads don't feel competent to deal with an emotional daughter. Second, those same hormones bring on major physical changes that transform "Daddy's little girl" into a mature young woman. Suddenly, the days of innocent wrestling and tickling are gone. Fathers don't know where to put their arms. Conscientious fathers who rightfully want to treat their daughters with respect and honor at a time when their bodies are changing, sometimes make the mistake of backing off entirely. While wisdom and respect need to guide a father's actions, adolescent children—both sons and daughters—need the affection of their fathers just as much as ever.

Growing Up Fast

Puberty is not something a dad needs to "fix"; neither is it something he can run from. It's simply something he must recognize, understand, and approach proactively and with sensitivity. If ever a child needed a daddy's security, it's at this critical stage of physical and emotional development.

Just over 150 years ago, the average age of puberty was almost seventeen years. Today it is twelve years and dropping.[3]

The problem with this increased pace of physical development is that it has not been balanced by a corresponding increase in maturity.

When children go through the great physiological revolution of puberty at the tender age of twelve (some begin as young as nine), they don't yet have the maturity to handle the massive changes taking place in their bodies. Often they are frightened by being forced to grow up so soon. How can we expect them to deal with puberty's powerful sexual changes when they haven't reached the maturity level necessary to safely navigate those changes? That's like giving them the keys to a new car before they're old enough to get a driver's license!

Looking for Love in All the Wrong Places

Many adolescent girls find themselves bombarded with the attention of young men with wrong motives while suffering abandonment from the first man in their lives: Dad.

I'm convinced that a girl who reaches puberty has a physiological need to tune in to a male via simple, healthy, affectionate touch—and if she doesn't get that touch from her dad, she will look for it elsewhere. Too many young teenage girls are looking for love in all the wrong places when what they are really searching for is a father's healthy touch. They're not looking for sex; they're looking for affection. Poll after poll has shown that a female's number one need is for affection (which is largely communicated through tender touch in a nonsexual way). As fathers we can safeguard our daughters by meeting their need for male affection in a healthy and secure family setting.

Thankfully, by the time my daughters entered puberty, we had already established our tradition of regular together-time. The girls were already receiving lots of male affection from Dad. One-on-one special times functioned as catalysts to increase the affection quotient and the quality of all our times together. Because they got so much tender touch from Daddy, they never felt driven to look elsewhere for male affection.

Boys Need Hugs Too

The need for touch is probably greater in our daughters than in our sons, as evidenced by the fact that a woman's sense of touch is on average ten times more sensitive than a man's.[4] But that doesn't mean it's OK to back off from showing affection to our growing sons. Boys need a dad's touch too. Granted, that affection may display itself in a rougher, more aggressive way—for example, through wrestling, play-punching, bear hugs, or sweating together in a game of one-on-one basketball—but it communicates the same thing: "You are loved and special. I want you close to me. My heart is open to you."

We need to hug our sons—and keep on hugging them. Sadly, many adolescent boys develop wrong attitudes toward women and sex because their fathers are not secure enough to talk openly with them about sex and its place in a loving marriage relationship. As dads, we need to teach our sons— by word and by example—that there's a difference between healthy affection and sexual behavior. We need to guide them through their sexual development in a positive way and model healthy affection at home.

Beating Peer Pressure

Of course, dads aren't the only ones who have a tendency to back away from hugs when their kids hit teen age. Peer pressure often causes older boys and girls to pull away from maintaining a close relationship with Mom and Dad. When kids start backing away, dads have to work extra hard at keeping the love and affection flowing. While you need to be sensitive to teens' changing emotions and outlook, you also need to work at bridging the "generational gap" that can creep into your relationship. It's natural for kids to pull away at this time, so you'll have to be creative and diligent in your efforts to stay close to your kids. They need your love and affection at all ages!

Ultimately, touch is the loudest way we have to communicate love, acceptance, and security to our children. Let's tell our sons and daughters that we love them—with words, yes; but also through the language of a daddy's tender touch.

Let the word of Christ dwell in you richly as you teach and admonish one another with all wisdom.

—Colossians 3:16

The Miracle
in a Daddy's Words

On that breakthrough morning in the kitchen with Danica, I wrapped my arms around her. Then I began to whisper words to her that were straight from my heart. I could literally feel peace flowing into her soul, driving out confusion, doubt, and fear. Every word I spoke seemed to speed unhindered, straight into the treasure vault of her heart. I sensed her soul growing healthier and stronger.

In those moments I felt so grateful to be part of God's ingenious plan for my daughter. Even the naturally low timbre of my voice was part of his plan. As I spoke, Danica could feel as well as hear the deep vibrations, and that seemed to have a physiologically calming effect on her.

Years later I noticed the same calming effect on my grandson. When he was about one year old, I would hold him cheek to cheek and tell him about the great things he would do in life. The lower my voice got, the more he would rest in my arms and snuggle his cheek into mine. He liked the feeling of those deep vibrations. God gives dads a low voice for a reason!

As a father I regard the privilege of speaking life into my children's souls as nothing short of miraculous. Every daughter longs to hear her daddy whisper, "You're my princess. You'll always be my princess." Every son longs to hear his dad's low voice confirm, "You're my son. I'm proud of you."

As a pastor for whom words are a stock in trade, I've always been impressed by the tremendous power inherent in words. The old adage "Sticks and stones can break my bones, but words can never hurt me" is far from true. Words may not be able to break our physical bones, but they can cause great pain; and if allowed to, they can break our spirits.

A Matter of Life and Death

Solomon said, "Death and life are in the power of the tongue" (Proverbs 18:21 NKJV). The extent of that power depends not only upon the words themselves but also upon the one who speaks them.

To children, Daddy's words are perhaps the most potent words of all. What fathers say to their children is a matter of life and death—perhaps not in a physical sense but definitely in an emotional and spiritual sense. Just as every seed requires water to grow, every child requires loving words to grow. Kids need to hear words like, "I'm so glad you're my child." "I'm proud of you." "Out of all the people in the world, God chose the perfect child for me." Life-giving miracles are released when children hear these types of words of praise and affirmation from Dad.

Why are words so powerful? Because they have the ability to paint permanent pictures in our minds. Even though we hear words audibly, communication is fundamentally a visual experience. Our words function as paintbrushes. When we hear "white picket fence," for example, we immediately see in our minds a picture of a white picket fence.

The words that are spoken by the most important people *in* our lives paint the most important pictures *for* our lives. That is why the words spoken by a father in his children's formative years are so powerful. What children hear from Dad during their childhood years can produce images that are extremely hard to erase.

The words we speak reflect what we see, and what we see is heavily influenced by what we believe. If we believe our children are winners, our words will reflect that: "You can do it!" "You're the best!" If we believe our children are losers, our words will reflect that too: "Why can't you ever do it right?" "You'll never get it!" Our children develop their identities by looking into the mirror of our words. They paint for themselves the self-images we reflect to them.

Many daddy holes are the result of a dad's negative and critical words. Other daddy holes are the result of his silence.

If we believe our children are winners, our words will reflect that.

When it comes to children, silence is not golden! A lack of encouraging words speaks a loud message to kids. It conveys disinterest, disapproval—even rejection. In the absence of a father's vitally needed praise and affirmation, a child's spirit is starved of the one thing it needs to grow.

When children never hear Daddy say, "I'm proud of you," they believe the opposite: "I'm ashamed of you." A steady diet of negative words—or no words at all—emaciates a child's spirit, drying up hopes and dreams.

Of course, what a mother says matters too. But the truth is, children rarely question Mom's love and acceptance. They are much more likely to question Dad's. That makes what we speak—and what we don't speak—vitally important.

Speaking with Integrity

Our words need to be trustworthy, because our children will lean on them with all their expectation. They don't know how not to. Trust is inherent in children. They must be taught how *not* to trust. When we say that we will take our kids to the park, they see a picture of their future with us in the park and fully expect that it will come to pass. They trust what we say and build the future on it. When we don't keep our promises, that future is rocked.

Ultimately, our children's security and stability are dependent upon our integrity. That means we must have the strength of character to live up to our words, keep our promises, and follow our own rules. We can't say one thing and live another. Our children are watching, and the little things we do speak the loudest: whether we throw the trash out the window or wait and put it in the can; whether we return the shopping cart or leave it out in the parking lot for someone else to put away; whether we correct the cashier when she gives us too much change or keep the money for ourselves; whether we join in with gossip or refuse to talk badly about others behind their backs.

Integrity is one of the greatest gifts we can give our children. When our words are backed up by the integrity of our lives, they can be a powerful influence for good. If our words don't match up with what we do, however, the negative impact on our children can be just as powerful.

The Words We Do

Words don't always have to be spoken. Sometimes the things we *do* speak volumes. A number of years ago, as I was preparing a Father's Day message for my congregation, it struck me that fathers—not children—were the ones who should be most thankful on that day. We are the blessed ones who've been given the privilege of fathering these gifts from God that we call our sons and daughters.

I decided that I would show my thankfulness to my daughters by giving each of them a Father's Day card. I wrote a note inside each card, thanking the girls for the privilege of being their father and listing a multitude of specific and individualized reasons why each one was so special to me.

It wasn't until years later that I fully understood how much these cards meant to my daughters. I found out that one of my girls carried an old Father's Day card in her Day-Timer where she could see it every day.

Another thing that spoke volumes to my daughters was my annual Valentine's Day bouquet. Every February 14 I would call the local florist and have a bouquet of flowers delivered to each of the girls at school. Each arrangement would have a balloon attached that said, "I Love You." The girls came to expect that when Valentine's Day rolled around, one of their classes would be interrupted by a florist delivering a special treat from Dad. Yes, they had to endure a little teasing from their classmates each time, but they got the message: They were special!

From Policeman to Coach

To a son or daughter setting out on the path of life, Daddy's words are powerful. They're like jet fuel in a combustion engine. A child can go a long way on a few timely words of positive encouragement from Dad.

I remember noticing the transformation that my positive words always seemed to generate when our girls were small. If I complained about their messy bedrooms, for example, my words tended to fall on deaf ears. But when I looked for opportunities to praise and encourage them as they worked to make their rooms presentable, my positive words seemed to spark them to multiply their efforts.

> *By choosing to see the potential for success in my children, my words began to paint a picture that empowered them for that success.*

As a result, as my girls got older, I found my role in their lives changing. I was less and less a policeman, concerned about setting and enforcing a code of conduct, and more and more a coach, cheering them on to reach their fullest potential.

Instead of looking for what they might be doing wrong, I started focusing more on what they could be doing right. By choosing to see the potential for success in my children, my words began to paint a picture that empowered them for that success.

I believe every dad is meant to be a coach. It's our job to speak words that say we believe in our children and see things for them beyond what they see for themselves. It's our job to cheer them on to stretch and reach for their highest goals. And as good coaches, it's our job to keep them focused on the path God has set before them so they don't go off in an unhealthy direction when they reach a tempting fork in the road.

Courage for a Generation

Words of encouragement build courage in the hearer; and if ever there was a generation that needed courage—the inner strength to do the right thing, even in the face of fear or ridicule—it's this one. Our children face temptations and challenges today that were unheard of when we were their age.

Society's solution is simple, but fundamentally flawed:

Lower your expectations. For example, instead of believing that children can overcome the bombardment of sexual temptations rampant in our world today, society compromises and says, "Go ahead and have sex. Just keep it safe." The fact is, there is no such thing as safe sex outside the totally monogamous lifestyle called marriage. Society is way off-base.

Instead of lowering the bar, we need to believe our children can successfully rise to whatever challenges face them. They will need great courage to do so, and that's where we come in. As dads we have the privilege and the responsibility to build courage in the hearts of our sons and daughters. Our role is to empower them to succeed by giving them heaps of encouragement through the words we speak each day.

Let's make it our goal to never let our children leave the house in the morning without a full tank of courage! After all, it's not hard to speak positive words. They're free and unlimited in quantity. They're impossible to overdo. And best of all, they're fully capable of working miracles in our children's lives.

These commandments that I give you
today are to be upon your hearts.
Impress them on your children. Talk
about them when you sit at home and
when you walk along the road, when
you lie down and when you get up.

—Deuteronomy 6:6–7

The Miracle in a Daddy's Time

It takes time to hug a child. But when a daddy hugs his child and lets the hug hold on—when he doesn't rush to release it but lets it take as much time as it takes—the result can be nothing short of miraculous.

I've thought a lot about this since that morning in the kitchen, when I hugged Danica and kept on hugging. I believe that when we take the time to wrap our arms around our children, it's as if we're wrapping them with our very lives. By our actions we say, "You are at the center of my life, and all that I am is dedicated to raising you to be strong, healthy, and secure."

The proof of our dedication is in our time. When we invest

time in our children, we tell them, "I love you." Time, after all, is the currency of life. We measure our lives by the accumulation of time that we are physically alive and by what we do and accomplish in that time. Our commitment to loving our families is measured by time as well—by the amount of quality time we spend with them.

Many dads complain that they don't have enough hours in the day to dedicate a significant portion to their children. The truth is, we all have the same twenty-four hours to work with. The key is planning. So often our intended priorities don't match our real priorities because we don't plan. Meanwhile, our real priorities are on display for all to see, imprinted in the concrete of our track record.

Time is the currency of life.

Children are observant; they know whether they're important to us or not. Dads who tell their children they love them but make no time for them are recognized by their kids for what they are: liars. Granted, some seasons of our lives and careers are busier than others. But a wise daddy will always find a balance that ensures he has time for his children.

The life Helen and I lead has always been busy. To be honest, I like it that way. But we've learned that the best way to avoid the tyranny of urgency is to plan for the important. Our family has been able to flourish in the midst of our many endeavors because of proper planning.

As I said in an earlier chapter, when my daughters were growing up, I made it a point to set aside time each month for special times with each of them. In addition to those individual times together, we also set aside every Thursday night as "family night." We all looked forward to Thursday nights and put in suggestions for things to do together. Often we went swimming or bowling. Sometimes we went out for pizza. Other times we stayed home and played games. Whatever the activity, we made sure our time together was focused, quality family time.

Breaking Bread Together

Most families have at least one opportunity for family togetherness each day: mealtime. The time we spend at the dinner table is the perfect family time. After all, everyone has to eat! In his book *Achieving Success without Failing Your Family*, Paul

Faulkner confirms that a common denominator among successful people with successful families is their commitment to a family mealtime.[1]

Unfortunately, families that sit down and eat dinner together are becoming quite rare. Recently, my wife heard an appalling statistic: Forty percent of meals eaten in North America are consumed on the run at fast-food restaurants. I don't know who came up with that number, but if it's true—and if we factor in the tendency of many families to let TV provide the dinner conversation at home—then very few meaningful family meals are taking place anymore.

That's too bad, because parents and children need regular times together to connect and enjoy one another's company and conversation. The "law of association" says that people associate their feelings with the people they are with at the time of their feeling. Eating a good meal is enjoyable. When we share a meal with our families, we associate those good feelings with our family members, and the good feelings extend to them too.

Regular family mealtimes have always been a priority in our home. They've definitely been a factor in developing healthy relationships between Helen and me and our daughters. Eating our meals together has taken planning, effort, and commitment, but the result has been well worth it.

Helen and I both grew up in families where mealtime was unquestionably family time. I have five brothers and five sisters, and our dinners together were always an experience, to say the least. Helen has two brothers and a sister, and their meals were also very lively. Around the dinner table, we would hear and share all the family news of the day. This would help us stay connected to one another, from the youngest family member to the oldest. It also helped us learn and practice our group communication skills!

To this day Helen and I still enjoy our meals with our extended families, although the number of family members around the table has grown quite a bit. At last count, the number at a Burns family dinner—which includes my mom and dad, my siblings, and their families—has climbed to fifty-eight. Now *that's* an experience!

Being Spontaneous

As we've said, the key to having time for our children is to plan for it. But that doesn't mean we shouldn't be spontaneous sometimes. I found that as I was diligent to plan for special times with my daughters, all the other times we had together became more special. Our one-on-one times together, family nights, and mealtimes acted as catalysts that raised the quality level of all our interactions.

My girls tell me that while they loved our planned times, some of their most beloved memories are of the more spontaneous times we spent together. They reminded me of some of them when we were on our most recent daddy-daughter trip. (I started the tradition of the daddy-daughter trip after our third daughter got married. Once a year I invite my three grown girls to join me for a minivacation to a city in North America. I let them choose the city, and we go there—just the four of us—for a few days. Over the years we've visited places like New York, Montreal, and San Diego. We've enjoyed great restaurants, great theater, and of course, great shopping.)

On our most recent daddy-daughter trip, I watched the little girl in each of my daughters bubble up as they relived some of their favorite childhood memories. One memory was of the number of times I came home from work too late to have tucked them into bed. Wanting some time with them, I would wake them up and take them in their pajamas to the local 7-Eleven store for giant Slurpees. It was a crazy thing to do—but they loved it, and so did I!

Their favorite family vacation was a spontaneous trip we took to Disneyland. I was driving the girls to school on the last day before spring break when I musingly asked, "What do you want to do on your week off?" Our youngest daughter, Ashley, who was about eight years old, chirped, "Let's go to Disneyland!" We all laughed and left it at that. Or so they thought.

That Sunday night after we got home from church, Helen and I told the girls to put on their pajamas and get in the van. As we pulled away from the house, they asked, "Where are we going?" When I answered, "Disneyland," they erupted with screams of glee that continued for the rest of the week.

With our van prepacked with essentials (plus a lot of junk food), we drove nonstop through the night, all the way from Vancouver to Anaheim. For the next several years, a nonstop Sunday-night drive to Disneyland for spring break was another family tradition.

Quality Follows Quantity

When it comes to the time we spend with our children, quality definitely follows quantity. Many dads think they can make up for the lack of time they spend with their children by offering a lesser amount of time and promising that it will be "quality time." But relationships don't work that way. A husband who tells his spouse, "Listen, honey, I've only got five minutes, so let's make it good," is not going to get anywhere with his wife. And a dad who promises, "I only have an hour on Saturday, but we'll make it quality time," isn't going to get anywhere with his kids.

We can't legislate quality time with our sons and daughters. We can't manufacture those special, golden moments that open our eyes to miracles. Those quality moments come on their own, unexpectedly, in the midst of the quantity time we dedicate to our children.

When our girls were small, I would tuck them into bed almost every night. I'd read part of a book to them, pray with them, give them a kiss, and turn out the light. I planned my evenings so I could have that special time with them on a regular basis.

I'll never forget one particular night when one of the girls interrupted my reading. "Daddy, how did you and Mommy fall in love?" she asked.

I laid the book down and watched my daughters' eyes dance with joy as I told them the story of their parents' romance. With my words I painted the picture of an amazing young lady named Helen and a clumsy, stuttering boy named John. I described what it felt like for us to be smitten with love for one another and later for our three little princesses. As I spoke I sensed their hearts snuggling up under the comfort and security of their parents' love. It was one of those spontaneous, golden moments that births miracles.

The Most Important Time

Thinking about the love between a mom and dad reminds me of an important point. It's true that fathers need to make time in their busy schedules for their children. But every daddy needs to remember: The most important time he can give his children is the time he gives his wife. A strong marriage builds the kind of strong home kids need in order to grow up healthy and secure.

chapter five

When our girls were young, Helen and I enjoyed a daily ritual we called our *p-and-q* time. This was our peace-and-quiet time. With a cup of our favorite coffee in hand, we would tell the girls we were going to have a little p-and-q time, and they would scamper off into another room. During this special time, Helen and I would update

Children love it when they know that Mom and Dad love each other and love God!

each other about what was going on in our lives. We would open our Bibles, share what we had read that morning, and talk about what God was teaching us. Little did we know that these times of sharing spiritual insights with one another would become the foundation on which we would start our ministry. Our p-and-q time was our seminary!

Inevitably, we would end our p-and-q time with our eyes closed, hands joined, praying. When we would open our eyes, we'd usually find three little girls gathered around our feet, smiling. Children love it when they know that Mom and Dad love each other and love God!

Friends Love at All Times

In healthy families, children are not the only things that grow. So do friendships.

Our friends are the people we like to spend time with. In healthy families, family members like each other; they like to spend time together. Family friendship is the connection that brings children home again long after they've grown up. It's what makes them *want* to come home when they no longer *need* to come home.

Friends influence our lives because we listen to them more than we listen to others. When we need counsel and advice, we go to friends, because we know we're safe with them. That's why, as fathers, we should want to be on the top of our children's lists. If our heart's desire is for our children to come to us first for counsel and advice, we must build the safety of friendship into our families. Only in a safe place, among friends, will children risk revealing their hopes, uncovering their fears, and exploring their dreams.

Helen and I regard our friendships with our children as treasure. We are thrilled that our daughters want to spend time with us and with each other. In fact, after our three girls were married, they decided they wanted to continue our family nights. Now, every Monday night they congregate with their families at our house. These are always special times of fun, storytelling, laughter, and love.

Recently, Helen and I spoke at a conference in Europe. On that Monday night, we phoned home to talk to our children. We called each of their houses, but no one answered. Then we called our house and discovered why: They were meeting at our home for family night. Even though we were out of the country, they didn't want to miss their time together.

The friendships we've developed in our family have opened the door for the girls to come to Helen and me for counsel and advice. What a tremendous compliment it is to have our children value our opinion enough to ask for it! I love hearing my daughters say, "Dad, I need your advice." And I love hearing them ask each other for advice; that lets me know they are friends with one another too.

Friendship with our children takes time; and in this day and age, time can be hard to come by. But every moment we spend with our sons and daughters is time well spent. We need to plan for those moments and enjoy them to the fullest. After all, there's a miracle in a daddy's time. When we invest our time in our children, a miracle happens in their hearts—and in ours.

God is love. Whoever lives in love lives in God, and God in him.

—1 John 4:16

The Miracle in a Daddy's Love

As I hugged Danica and held her close to my heart that special morning, I sensed that something powerful was happening. I knew that she was literally feeling and hearing my heartbeat. But more importantly I could tell that, as if through osmosis, she was receiving the message of my heart: "Daddy loves you unconditionally, and nothing you can do will ever change that."

The most valuable treasure a dad has to offer his children is the gift of unconditional love.

I knew I had to get what was in my heart into my daughter's heart. There was a miracle of love, peace, confidence, and health in my heart that she desperately needed. For years Danica had been trying to do something to make me love her more while being afraid of doing something that would make me love her less. What she needed was the freedom to simply be herself. Somehow I had to convincingly communicate to her that my love for her was forever and would never change.

She needed a revelation of unconditional love.

Unconditional love is miraculous. It is the superpower of the universe. God is love, and his love is always unconditional. As the apostle Paul stated, "Love never fails" (1 Corinthians 13:8). It can overcome anything.

Shame and guilt lose their tyranny, and fear has no power in the face of a daddy's unconditional love.

A daddy's love should always be unconditional. That's the birthright of every child. It shouldn't have to be earned, and it must never be the reward for a job well done. Nothing can alienate a child quicker than having to work for something that should be freely given.

But when children know that they are unconditionally loved by Dad, they know they can never lose. If they fall, they can get back up and keep going. Shame and guilt lose their tyranny, and fear has no power in the face of a daddy's unconditional love.

The Soil of Unconditional Love

Every seed needs the right soil to develop to its fullest potential. As we've said before, children are miracles in seed form. What is the best soil for their optimum growth? Unconditional love. Children need to be surrounded with unconditional love in order to blossom into the miracles God intends for them to be.

A daddy's hug is a physical illustration of soil wrapped around a seed. But that soil is much more than physical arms. It's more than audible words. It's a father's very heart. The way we look at our children, talk to our children, think of our children, pray for our children—all of these make up the soil of unconditional love that wraps securely around the miracle seeds we call our sons and daughters.

That morning in the kitchen, as I wrapped my arms lovingly around my daughter, a wonderful miracle took place. Danica was able to draw hope and healing from the wells of my heart. Like a seed sprouting with new life, her own heart began to open up and breathe.

"I love you," I whispered. "Nothing you can ever do can make me love you more, and nothing you can ever do can make me love you less." My words were like a spring rain, gently watering the miracle that was unfolding before me.

But Danica wasn't the only one who experienced a miracle that day. I realized that I had been trying for years to do something to help my daughter get free while being afraid of doing something that might bind her even more. I needed the revelation of unconditional love too. The miracle in a daddy's hug set us both free.

The Conditions of Unconditional Love

Unconditional love is unchangeable. By definition, it is unaffected by the conditions in which it finds itself. We must love our children the same amount and to the same degree, no matter what challenges or conditions confront us.

It's easy to show love when everything is going great. It takes commitment, however, to love in the face of challenging conditions. In fact, it is only through the storms and struggles of life that the commitment to love unconditionally really manifests itself.

Children know intuitively that what is not tested cannot be trusted. Many times what we identify as "bad behavior" is simply our kids testing our love to discover whether or not it is trustworthy. Children will go to great lengths to test the commitment of their parents' love for them and for each other, to the point of manufacturing conditions that test that love. I call these the *conditions* of unconditional love. In the presence of conditions, unconditional love—or the lack thereof—becomes crystal-clear.

Many times what we identify as "bad behavior" is simply our kids testing our love to discover whether or not it is trustworthy.

Unconditional Love in Marriage

When a mom and dad have unconditional love for one another, they provide a sure foundation for their children's lives. Marriage is the commitment of a husband to unconditionally love his wife forever and the reciprocal commitment of his wife to love her husband forever. Out of the overflow of this unconditional love, a healthy family is birthed.

Children evaluate the strength of their parents' love for them in light of the strength of their parents' love for one another. They think, *If something can change the love between Mom and Dad, how do I know that something won't change their love for me?* If a mom and dad decide that they no longer love each other, the soil of unconditional love is breached, and the miracle seed is exposed and vulnerable.

In her groundbreaking study on the impact of divorce on children, Judith S. Wallerstein followed the development of children of divorce for twenty-five years following their parents' breakups. To her surprise, Wallerstein found that the harshest effects of divorce don't emerge until children reach adulthood. She writes in her book *The Unexpected Legacy of Divorce*:

> Those from intact families found the example of their parents' enduring marriage very reassuring when they inevitably ran into marital problems. But in coping with the normal stresses in a marriage, adults from divorced families were at a grave disadvantage. Anxiety about relationships was at the

bedrock of their personalities and endured even in very happy marriages. Their fears of disaster and sudden loss rose when they felt content. And their fear of abandonment, betrayal, and rejection mounted when they found themselves having to disagree with someone they loved.[1]

Children of divorce lack the firm foundation of parents who love one another unconditionally. They learn through painful experience to distrust the invisible fiber of commitment. As a result, they often find it hard to trust others. They have trouble feeling secure and stable, especially in relationships.

Their sense of identity and belonging is shaken; and in their ensuing search for identity and acceptance, they often become trapped on a performance treadmill. Based on Mom and Dad's model, they believe that love is ultimately conditional—that whatever love they receive from others will always be dependent upon what they do or don't do.

When Children Leave the Nest

Of course, none of us is perfect in showing unconditional love. Every family goes through challenges. But it is during such times that we discover the strength of our foundation.

As a dad, one of my toughest challenges has been to walk my daughters down the aisle and give them away in marriage. In each of these events, and in the events that led up to them, my level of unconditional love was tested. Did I love my daughters enough to let them go?

Our oldest daughter, Angela, was the first to get married. When her boyfriend, Rod, met me for coffee at Starbucks and asked me for Angela's hand in marriage, I was surprised at my emotional reaction. To his question, "May I have your daughter's hand in marriage?" I tearfully replied, "Yes, you can be her husband, but I will always be her dad!" (The tears didn't stop for three days. I had to wear sunglasses to hide my puffy, red eyes.)

Obviously, I was not prepared to handle such an important moment rationally. With my brain on the blink, I told Rod that I would race him home so he could ask Angela right away. It never dawned on me that he might have had some romantic escapade planned so he could ask her to marry him at the perfect place and time.

We left Starbucks, jumped into our separate cars, and got to the house at about the same time. I ran in the back door, blubbering to Helen that Rod and Angela were getting married, while Rod ran in the front door calling for Angela. It was just before bedtime, so Angela came hurrying down the stairs in oversized flannel pajamas, her hair up in a ponytail, and her face covered in cream stuff.

Hearing the commotion, Angela's sisters peered out of their bedrooms, and Helen and I peeked around the kitchen corner as Rod got down on one knee at the bottom of the stairs. He looked up at Angela and asked her to marry him. When he gave her the engagement ring, we all cheered and cried. It was a complete family affair! I suppose the moment wasn't quite as romantic as Rod and Angela might have liked, but it's a memory none of us will ever forget.

On the eve of Angela's wedding, emotions ran high. Helen, Angela, and I were acutely aware that life as we knew it was about to change forever. We were experiencing the closure of a season of life—the season of Angela living at home in her frilly bedroom full of dolls and girly things. That night Angela sobbed uncontrollably in her mother's arms. "I know this is good, but it hurts so much," she cried over and over.

We knew the pain Angela was feeling was good pain. It

came from love. If she hadn't loved her family and her life at home so much, leaving wouldn't have hurt so much. Helen and I were hurting too.

But God's plan is for our children's lives to keep getting better. They're *supposed* to move from the wonderful season of growing up in a loving family and happy home to a better season of building their own loving marriages, families, and homes. And the fact is, to grasp this better future, they must let go of the past—however frightening and painful that might be.

Where do they find the unchangeable strength they need to get through the pain and difficulty of such a monumental change? In Mom and Dad's unconditional love.

An Unforgettable Wedding Day

On Angela's wedding day, my job was not only to walk her down the aisle and offer her hand in marriage to Rod; it was also to perform the ceremony. Some of my friends thought I wouldn't be able to do it all—the daddy stuff *and* the pastor stuff—because I would get too emotional.

"It's my party, and I'll cry if I want to," I told them. Then

I made sure to plan the ceremony in a way that would make the emotional times easier to deal with.

So I walked Angela down the aisle as a proud father, following the traditional service up to the point when the minister typically asks, "Who gives this woman to be married to this man?" Since there was no presiding minister on the platform to ask the question (he was busy being the dad!) I turned to Angela and lifted her veil.

"Angela," I said, "nineteen-and-a-half years ago, God blessed your mother and me with true sunshine when Angela Sunshine was born to us. You became the center of our lives, and we love you so much. Everything we have done has been in preparation for this decision you are making today. We believe you are well equipped to be a great wife and mother."

I turned to Rod. "Rod, for the past nineteen-and-a-half years we have been praying for the man that God would prepare to be the perfect husband for Angela," I said. "We now know we have been praying for you." Then I took Angela's hand, put it in his, and continued, "I give you the hand of our daughter in marriage, and Helen and I welcome you into our family."

Of course I was very emotional during this whole spiel. Tears flowed freely. Once I finished speaking, however, I gathered myself together, walked up onto the platform, and began to perform the rest of the ceremony.

Everything went normally until the wedding-ring part. At that point I took Angela's hand, which already had a ring on the third finger, and said, "Angela, on your seventeenth birthday, your mom and I gave you this ring as a symbol of a covenant we made with you that day. You resolved, with God's help, to keep yourself holy and chaste until that day when you would walk down this aisle, committing your life in marriage to the man God had prepared for you.

"I take this covenant ring off your finger to make room for a better covenant."

"We want to thank you for being faithful to that covenant. God will bless you and your marriage all the days of your life. Now I take this covenant ring off your finger to make room for a better covenant."

I removed the ring from her finger, paving the way for Rod's ring to replace it. A few minutes later, I had the privilege and great blessing of declaring Angela and Rod husband and wife.

That night, after the newlyweds left for their honeymoon, I found a special treasure on my pillow. It was a thank-you note from Angela. Let me share it with you:

Dad,

I didn't know how to write this and stay composed. I feel like my heart is broken right now. I know that this is good—I'm moving on and I'm doing the right thing, but it hurts so much.

I want you to know that I love you so much. I'll always be your daughter. Thank you for being a gentle, wonderful daddy when I was a little girl and for doing everything you could to stick with it when I became a teenager. Thank you for being "Dad" before "Pastor" and for showing me exactly what my husband should be like.

I will never forget all of the wonderful memories we have—the fishing trips and dates and family vacations. You are the best daddy a girl could ask for, and I love you very, very much. I know that our relationship will only grow from here.

I love you, Dad.

Angela Sunshine Burns

All three of our daughters had glorious weddings full of celebration and love. Each of their ceremonies included the removal of the covenant rings Helen and I had given them on their seventeenth birthdays—symbols of our partnering with them as they navigated the journey from adolescence to the altar. The rings weren't removed until they were ready to be replaced by rings of a better covenant.

Each of our daughters left us a note of thanks after their weddings. I keep these treasures with me wherever I go. They remind me of the true riches of life—and the miraculous power of unconditional love.

As dads, we need to make a commitment to love our children (and our wives) fully, completely, and without conditions. Such love has great power, because it's the kind of love God has for each of us. Let's surround our children with the soil of unconditional love—and watch the miracles grow!

Faith is being sure of what
we hope for and certain of
what we do not see.

—Hebrews 11:1

The Miracle in a Daddy's Faith

What a father believes about his child is powerful. A daddy's faith in his son or daughter—if communicated effectively—has the power to produce a healthy, confident child who is motivated to work toward a positive future.

We can't see faith, but it has substance. The Bible defines faith as "the substance of things hoped for, the evidence of things not seen" (Hebrews 11:1 NKJV). When we as dads have faith *in* our kids and *for* our kids, we have something of substance to offer them. We have a confident hope that harbors no doubts or fears about their future. They can grasp that faith, take it into their hearts, and make it their own.

As I prayed about Danica and her eating disorder, God gave me a supernatural confidence. He gave me the faith to believe the best about my daughter and for my daughter. Out of that faith came a miracle—a miracle that started in God's heart, for he knew Danica's future and had no doubts or fears about it. God was confident about his plans for her. That confidence spread from his heart to my heart, and then from my heart to Danica's heart through the miracle in a daddy's hug.

Because of that miracle, Danica's faith multiplied and her doubts and fears dissipated. She was filled with a vision of hope for her future. She still had to do the work that was necessary to bring to pass what she saw by faith. She was the only one who could change her world; God wasn't going to come down and do the work for her. But now she had the confidence to step out and believe that she could succeed. What's more, I had the confidence to let go and trust that with God's help, she could and would do the work necessary to beat the eating disorder and fulfill God's plan for her life.

A successful future is always designed with hope and built by faith. Faith prompts action; when we have faith, action naturally follows. Danica's newfound faith led her to employ body, soul, and spirit to bring her hoped-for future to pass. It wasn't easy, and it wasn't immediate. But she succeeded!

Faith Sees Differently

The miracle in a daddy's hug starts with a father seeing his child with the eyes of faith. Faith sees beyond the natural to the miraculous. Faith doesn't accept what is apparent; it stretches from what *is* to what *could be.*

The best way for us to grow this kind of faith-filled vision is to spend time with God. Jeremiah 29:11 says, "'For I know the plans I have for you,' says the Lord. 'They are plans for good and not for evil, to give you a future and a hope'" (TLB). God has a plan and a vision for our children. When we as dads spend time with God in prayer and Bible study, the vision God has for them becomes our vision. We begin to see our children as God does: as wise, strong, loving, creative, able, obedient, thankful, faithful, and joyful miracles with limitless potential.

Our children need to have eyes of faith too. They need to see good things for themselves and for their future. They need to see that, despite whatever difficulties they face, their present circumstances don't have to determine their future's outcome. They don't have to be just another statistic; they can be miracles, instead.

When our daughters were growing up, we made a habit of pointing out people who were doing great things with their lives and telling the girls that they could do the same things one day if they wanted to. We encouraged them to pursue their dreams. (A person of faith is a dreamer with a work belt on!)

We often asked them what they wanted to be when they grew up. In their answers they would always shoot for the stars. At one point our youngest daughter, Ashley, said she wanted to be a great singer like Darlene Zschech, the songwriter and worship leader for Hillsongs in Australia. She never let go of that dream, and one day she surprised us all.

She was about thirteen years old, and her youth group was singing on the platform during a Sunday-morning church service. Helen and I were happy to see Ashley's smiling face among the students. Our happiness turned to amazement, however, when Ashley stepped forward to sing a solo.

Where did she get a voice like that? We thought we knew our children! Didn't all three of them sing around the house all the time? But a new Ashley emerged when she stepped forward on the platform to minister. Her voice was strong, warm, and sure. It was as if she'd been singing solos for years.

In the years that followed, Ashley continued to pursue her dream. Today she heads up our church music department, and she is our main praise and worship leader. Because we saw Ashley with eyes of faith, she was able to see herself with eyes of faith too. Then she worked toward what she saw until it came to pass.

Faith Speaks Differently

Faith not only sees differently; it speaks differently. When we spend time with God, our faith is built up, and our words begin to emanate from hearts of faith. The words we speak to our children become different from the negative, discouraging words they hear every day from the world. Hebrews 11:3 says, "By faith we understand that the worlds were framed by the word of God, so that the things which are seen were not made of things which are visible" (NKJV). Our faith-filled words frame a different world for our children—a world that is positive, encouraging, and brimming with potential.

Words produce after their own kind. Words of faith produce

faith; words of fear produce fear. God holds us responsible for the words we speak, because they have such immense creative power. Jesus said, "But I say to you that for every idle word men may speak, they will give account of it in the day of judgment. For by your words you will be justified, and by your words you will be condemned" (Matthew 12:36–37 NKJV).

When the words we speak to our children come from hearts of faith, our children's hearts are empowered to believe in a positive future.

Our words to our children are particularly powerful. When the words we speak to our children come from hearts of faith, our children's hearts are empowered to believe in a positive future, and they are encouraged to build toward it. When our words come from hearts of doubt and fear, however, our children's hearts are crippled and rendered powerless against discouragement and the whims of circumstance.

When our girls were small, Helen and I taught them that

their words had power. We encouraged them to speak words of faith by having them memorize a list of truths that we'd drawn from the Bible. It became their daily confession. It went something like this: "I am a miracle full of miracles. I love and I am loved; I am blessed and I am a blessing. I have the mind of Christ, and my memory is blessed. Wisdom watches over me and keeps me safe. I can do all things through Christ Jesus who strengthens me."

Now that our daughters are married, we are busy speaking words of faith over our grandchildren and teaching them to speak these same faith-filled words over themselves. They've heard "You're so smart!" and "You're the best!" so many times, they know they are!

Faith Acts Differently

Hebrews 12:2 says that Jesus is "the author and finisher of our faith" (NKJV). When a daddy's heart is full of faith, his actions toward his children exemplify the actions of the author of faith. The more his faith grows, the more he models his actions on what Jesus would do in his place. Increasingly he finds himself motivated by the things he sees in his children with eyes of faith—those positive, eternal things that God sees in them, not the negative, temporal things he used to react to.

But his faith does more than influence his own actions; it greatly affects what his children believe about themselves and the actions they take as a result. It also affects what they believe about God and how they respond to him as their heavenly Father.

His faith does more than influence his own actions; it greatly affects what his children believe about themselves and the actions they take as a result.

The fact is, small children base their concept of God on their fathers. If their image of Dad is not positive, their relationship with God is often damaged for life. Many adults today can't grasp the concept of a loving, forgiving, gracious heavenly Father because of the negative actions of their earthly fathers when they were growing up.

As dads we have a responsibility to make sure our children develop a healthy concept of their Father in heaven. Recognizing this responsibility should drive us to God. The faith he gives us is what empowers us to act in ways that point our children toward him.

I'll be honest with you. I wish I had read a book like this before I hit the battleground of parenthood. When I first became a father, I'd never heard of dating your children. I'd never considered the power of touch or the power of words in raising kids. I had no idea how to transfer faith from my heart to a child's heart. I didn't know there was a miracle in a daddy's hug. Discovering these things was a direct result of the faith God put in my heart as I spent time with him in prayer and the study of his Word.

The Power of Faith

God created us to live by faith. He is pleased when we do so, and he is pleased when we teach our children to do so. Hebrews 11:6 says it's impossible to please God without faith. Living by faith is the most exciting life possible; when we live by faith, we experience the abundant life that Jesus came to bring us (see John 10:10). Our faith touches the heart of God and releases all the resources of heaven to bring miracles to pass.

As our girls were growing up, they never tired of hearing the story of how faith produced a miraculous turnaround in their parents' marriage. Hearing about Mom and Dad's faith in God—and the blessings that flowed from it—helped them choose the life of faith for themselves.

Here's the story we told: Many years ago our marriage was in trouble. Most nights Helen cried herself to sleep out of loneliness. We didn't know how to communicate with one another, and I had an acute stuttering problem that only made matters worse.

In desperation Helen cried out to God. Afterward, as she opened her Bible, God began to reveal his will for her. (Faith always starts when the will of God is revealed!) God's words began to paint a new picture in her heart. Instead of seeing herself as a failure, she began to see what God saw: an amazing, lovely, talented woman, brimming with potential. What God believed began to rub off on her, and her every action began to reflect her new faith.

A few days later, she prayed, "God, I know you love my husband, so can you show me why? Please show me what you see in him, because I'm having trouble seeing anything good."

Then, as she searched her Bible again, God's words began to paint a new picture of her husband. Instead of seeing me as reclusive and fearful, she began to see what God saw: a loving husband and father who would sit in a place of leadership and make a difference in the world.

From that point on, when she talked to me, her words were different. Her faith spoke a new language. I began to see what she saw, and the faith that filled her heart with hope began to grow in my heart too. Soon my actions reflected my new faith, and my life totally changed. Our marriage and family have been flourishing ever since.

Children need to hear stories like this. They need to hear about their parents' faith. They need to see that faith in action, and they need to know the miracles that result from it. On this foundation their own faith walk is built—and miracles follow.

I hope you've found *The Miracle in a Daddy's Hug* to be an inspiring, practical message. As we've said, every child is a miracle full of miracles—a precious seed with the DNA for greatness inside. In the miracle soil of a daddy's hug, that greatness is able to blossom and flourish.

Why? Because a daddy's hug incorporates his touch, his words, and his time. It communicates his love and his faith. All these ingredients combine to create the right environment for a miracle to take place in a child's life—and in a daddy's life too.

A daddy's hug is simple and portable. It's weightless and convenient. It's powerful, durable, limitless, expandable, applicable, enjoyable, and free. And best of all, it works! So go ahead, wrap your arms around your child. Don't hold back. Don't ever stop. Hug and keep on hugging.

And watch for a miracle.

Notes

Chapter 3: The Miracle in a Daddy's Touch

1. Charles Faraone, *Let's Hug* (New York: Planet Books, 1983, 1995). Used by permission.

2. Marilyn Elias, "A Hands-On Approach: Touch Therapy Feels Its Way to the Forefront," *USA Today,* May 28, 1996.

3. Archibald Hart, *The Sexual Man* (Nashville: Thomas Nelson/W Publishing Group, 1995), 43.

4. Allan and Barbara Pease, *Why Men Don't Listen and Women Can't Read Maps* (London: Orion Publishing Group, 2001), 40.

Chapter 5: The Miracle in a Daddy's Time

1. Paul Faulkner, *Achieving Success without Failing Your Family* (West Monroe, La.: Howard Publishing Company, 1994), 340.

Chapter 6: The Miracle in a Daddy's Love

1. Judith S. Wallerstein, *The Unexpected Legacy of Divorce* (New York: Hyperion Press, 2001), 300.